# SACCADES

*poems by*

# Paul Long

*Finishing Line Press*
Georgetown, Kentucky

# SACCADES

## ACKNOWLEDGMENTS

A few of the poems appeared in Big Allis, Ribot, and First Intensity




Publisher: Leah Huete de Maines
Editor: Christen Kincaid
Cover Art: Paul Long
Author Photo: Clara Long
Cover Design: Elizabeth Maines McCleavy


Order online: www.finishinglinepress.com
also available on amazon.com

Author inquiries and mail orders:
Finishing Line Press
PO Box 1626
Georgetown, Kentucky 40324
USA

# Contents

# SPEAKING AS AN ENGINE

because you hold out for the flawless edge

a horizon forms
on your sleeve

Yet a rest in music

figure in white on the bed
suggesting poetry is sounds

or a souvenir

I type limits can be language

the way a name is attached

to something
by the tongue     after naming it

you explain summer concentrated you

a rasping of noise between limbs

like water your surface contracting


my mouth could be a bridge
with silence as the cables


to make tracks
the human remains


up or down

my arms bruised by your breathing

acting on landscape
as with sex

low clouds extend the focus

I pass knee to belly
flesh to pale fruit

to separate static figures
as a word

Among trees
your body through a lens

delicate     this margin
the strip surprises you

symbol responding

I suggested to lie down

your equivalent a tunnel

      imagined correctly or incorrectly
      the summer is still one texture


yet you seem to know

      as you follow with your finger

# CRYSTALLINE PROCEDURAL

she produces within her mouth

her relationship to him

a famous photographer


Volume could be a character of definition


The formal device regarding beauty is exercised
experience like clothes around the body


emphasize repetition


a finger visiting the same season

on the verge of lips

he came to gain confidence

being a figure of water


she sees herself
in the reflection


his hand open over the table


instead of vanishing
he sorts this relationship with coincidence


her language now a piece of white silk

Careful not to lure a fog

her barefeet shape

what he sees


    mixture of saliva and oil


undressing
    a row of footlights
    when she enters


his desire

    a similar migration

she walks through rooms

      exaggerating the experience


this conversation like her hand

      a crossing-guard

      to


this device


      almost        a scratch
      instinctive    strategy

      so erotic      the visual part


Formal at the emotional horizon

under control
      the after image of himself

# CENTRIPETAL SIGNS

you think of home

    across this distortion


    a demand to unify
    discontinuous affections


Structure identified with order


In the corridor I wait
    an inferred line

    that appears to speed up


the space of your desire

from conscious recognition

your figure immobile
is the color of sky


I appear in the middle of an errand


      over the carpet I sing
      love


you are finished counting
      at stake is not location


night gives the impression of your body

to begin

exposure is unspecified

a stamped involvement

you may appear

on the bed
in form your body diagonal

your breasts absorb space

or your voice is emotionally distant

this measure

        your structure
a large apartment


for me
it is a rhythm


making love to the size of your body

fireworks on a television screen


       space
           now

between fatigue and relief of accommodation

I have exaggerated you
      to a symbolic center


Accompanying dancers clear the foliage


my life protects itself
                its repetition



I understand the eye's passage
              the trace of light

     your name

          a planet at the edge

from the inner gate
      you digest the bridge


       piece


your achievement is not remembering


       passing
    time binds itself


a reflecting surface provided

for the experience of your unfinished occupation

# SUBORDINATED IS SOUND

he can only see the fringe

or prefers to lie down

it becomes the dominant force
from her mouth

the glass


this is a breakthrough
and she is careful
wrapping herself in vanilla



billowing
it is easy to make tracks on

here it darkens for her return


       his limited dance
       or a line of rocks


softening the body
one could say

           a chute


delicate would be fog

she pauses

waiting for him
to move

the rest can be correspondingly inferred

Graceful as a tunnel

she turns
heavier in the seduction

darker than others he melts

leaning beneath this stomach
the edge of her hand a camera lens

the monotony of this movement
                    confuses


she would say she has already eaten


          Symmetry is not produced
          by doing something and
          then doing it backward



This conversation
          he explains



                    is


                    filling the gap


          the part of the body
          behind the hand
          she can't see

**Paul Long** lives and teaches in Baltimore, MD. His poems have appeared in *Rhizome, Poetry New York, First Intensity, American Letters & Commentary, Fence,* and the *Sonoma Review.* His collection, *A Piece of Wood Drawn from Memory,* was a finalist for the National Poetry Series. Current projects include a collection of linked poems and letters about P.T. Barnum, focusing on his days at the famed American Museum in New York City, and a lyrical sequence about the virgin huntress Artemis, and her brief encounter with the fabled hunter Actaeon.

www.ingramcontent.com/pod-product-compliance
Lightning Source LLC
Chambersburg PA
CBHW022102080426
42734CB00009B/1462